MUMMIES: UNWRAPPING THE PAST

ROSALIE DAVID

WEIDENFELD & NICOLSON
LONDON

The word 'mummy' was originally used to describe the preserved bodies of ancient Egyptians. It comes from the Persian word 'mumia', meaning 'pitch' or 'bitumen', a substance believed to flow from mountains in the Near East. Bitumen from the famous 'Mummy Mountain' in Persia was believed to cure diseases, and when demand exceeded supply, people turned to the preserved bodies of the ancient Egyptians, whose blackened appearance was believed to indicate that they had the same medical powers as the *mumia*, and their skin tissue was used in medicine from medieval times until the 19th century. Thus, the word 'mummy' came to be used for these bodies, and still describes a body (skeleton and body tissues) that is naturally or artificially preserved.

Mummified head, showing preservation of tissue. Egyptian mummification has produced the best results (c.1900 BC, British Museum).

What is a mummy?

Mummies are found in many countries, and can be preserved in many ways. Some bodies are preserved by natural circumstances: this is called 'unintentional' or 'natural' mummification, because there has been no human intervention to achieve these results – the heat or cold of the climate, the dryness of the sand surrounding the body, and the absence of air in the burial can all contribute to the mummification process, and produce varying results.

But in some countries and civilizations people also played a part in this process and intentionally increased some of the natural conditions so that the body would be better preserved. They could exclude air by providing a sealed burial place, and use additional heat sources to dry out the body tissues so that they would not decompose. The ancient Egyptians took this technique still further, and used chemical substances and other means to prevent the decomposition of the body. It is this process that is called 'true mummification' and provides the best surviving examples of mummies.

Why did the Egyptians mummify their dead?

The religious beliefs and practices of the ancient Egyptians were directly influenced by the nature of the land and its climate. Herodotus, the famous Greek historian, described Egypt as the 'gift of the Nile', and it was the annual flooding of the river, rather than the scanty rainfall, which enabled some parts of the land to be cultivated. Although a vast area of Egypt is desert, the Delta (the triangle of land through which the Nile flows to reach the Mediterranean) and the Nile Valley are fertile because of the annual river flood which, until recent times, deposited rich black mud on the riverbanks. Using a series of

Body coffins of the Two Brothers, Khnum-Nakht and Nekht-Ankh. Rifeh, Egypt (c.1900 BC, Manchester Museum).

Valley of the Kings, Thebes, where the rulers of the New Kingdom (c.1500–1000 BC) were buried in rock-cut tombs.

canals, the ancient Egyptians were able to irrigate an area of land where they could grow food crops and rear their animals, and they built their towns and cities in this cultivated strip. They called this area 'Kemet', meaning the 'Black Land', because of the colour of the black soil. However, beyond these fertile river banks, the desert stretched away to the horizon. The Egyptians regarded it as a place of death and terror and called it 'Deshret' (from which we get our own word 'desert'). This meant 'Red Land', and described the colour of the rocks and sand.

The Black and Red Lands symbolized both life and death, and fertility and emptiness for the Egyptians. These areas also provided the physical conditions which gave rise to mummification. The cultivable land was scarce and had to be used as a place for people to live, grow their crops and rear their animals. It was too valuable to be used for burials, and therefore, from as early as *c.* 5000 BC, it became the custom to place the dead in shallow graves on the edges of the desert where the heat of the sun and the dryness of the sand helped to preserve the body indefinitely. Before decomposition set in, the body

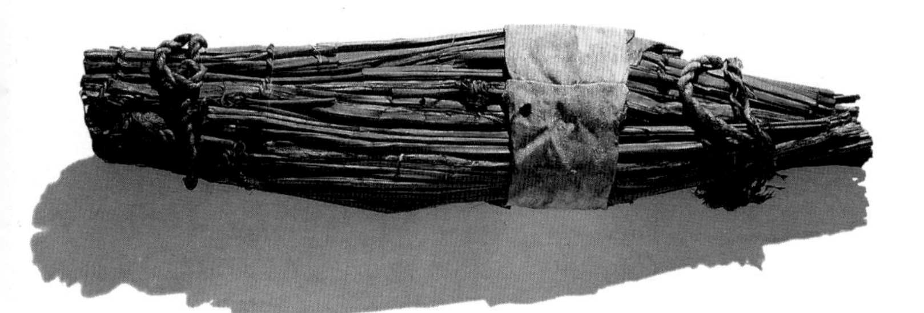

Mummy of a child wrapped in a reed mat; from Gurob, (c.1450 BC, Manchester Museum).

Early burials in shallow graves produced 'natural mummies' with preserved skin and hair (before 3100 BC, British Museum).

tissues were rapidly dried out, and the sand around the corpse absorbed the bodily fluids. These 'natural mummies' are often well preserved, and the skin and hair remain on the body. The shallow graves were probably later opened up, and the preserved bodies exposed to view, by wild animals such as jackals; thus, the families and descendants of the dead became aware that the bodies retained the appearance of their relatives when they were still alive.

From around 3400 BC the burial customs of the ruling classes began to change; they were now placed in brick-lined underground chambers instead of shallow graves in the sand, and because the corpses were no longer surrounded by the hot, dry sand, they rapidly decomposed. But because people had come to believe that a person's spirit survived after death and needed to be able to return to his body within the tomb, the spirit would have to be able to recognize this body so that it could enter it and take nourishment from the food offerings which were left at the tomb. So the Egyptians had to search for alternative methods of preserving the body and retaining the individual's appearance, and for several hundred years they experimented with a range of different techniques. By about 2600 BC they had developed the process we call 'true mummification'. This was used at first for royalty, but rapidly spread to the nobility and wealthier middle classes, and continued in use for these people until Islam became the main religion of Egypt after the Arabs invaded Egypt in 641 AD. Natural mummification (burial in shallow graves in the sand) continued to be used throughout this period for the poorer classes.

In the Middle Kingdom (*c.* 1900 BC), one of Egypt's most important gods – Osiris – became very powerful. Osiris was both god and king of the dead, and ruled his kingdom in the underworld, where men and women of all classes who had lived good lives were believed to continue their existence after death, cultivating the fields and crops in an eternal springtime. The annual death and rebirth of Osiris reflected the country's yearly death and revival when the flood restored the fertility of the parched land. The Egyptians believed that Osiris had been a human king who was murdered by his brother, but was ultimately restored to life as King of the Dead. After his murder, Osiris's limbs were torn apart and scattered all over Egypt, but his wife, Isis, gathered them together again, and his mummification was

Wooden panel showing the god of the dead, Osiris (front), and his wife, Isis (c.600 BC. Manchester Museum).

A panel portrait painted in the owner's lifetime and eventually placed on his mummy. Hawara, Egypt (c.200 BC, Manchester Museum).

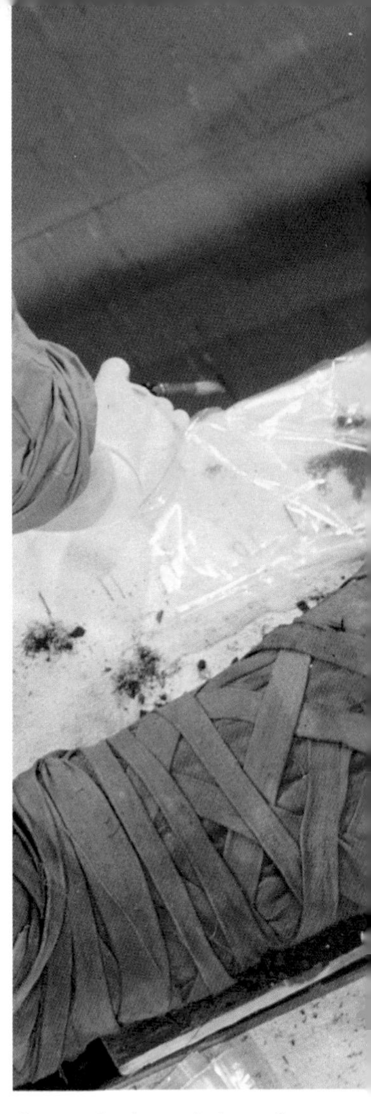

reputed to provide the pattern for the most expensive method, carried out for those who could afford it, which was believed to ensure their own rebirth.

It was at this time too that the funerary goods placed on the body and in the tomb became so important, and they became widely available to the middle classes. The body was wrapped in many layers of linen bandages, amongst which were placed amulets (sacred charms); it was then encased in a nest of coffins. There were usually two but sometimes three of these; the innermost

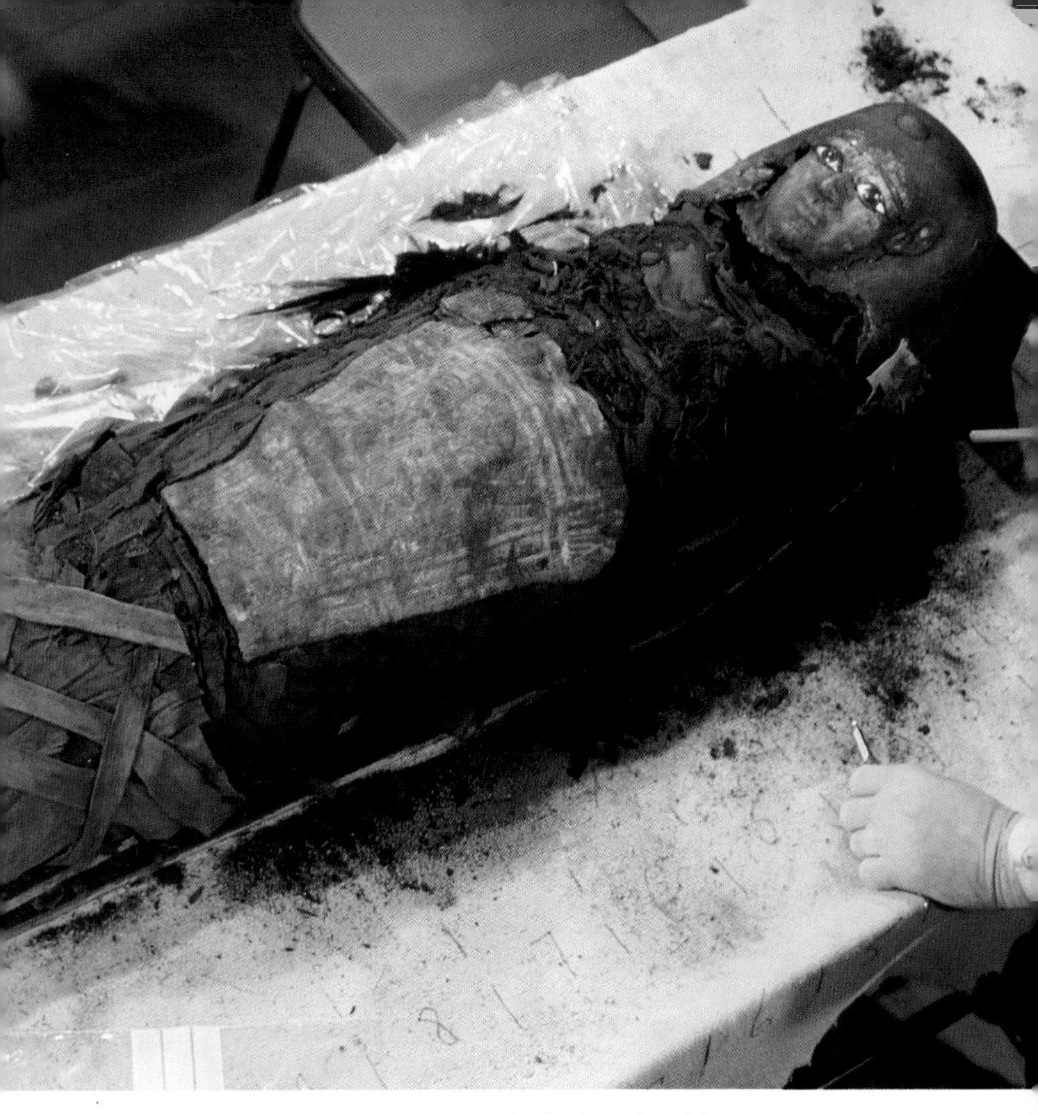

Mummy unwrapped at Manchester in 1975, showing gilded face mask and plaster chest cover (c.100 BC, Manchester Museum).

ones were body shaped and the outermost was rectangular. These mass-produced coffins were decorated with religious scenes and inscriptions and painted with stylized faces which did not depict the features of the individual owners. Later, in the Graeco-Roman period (*c.*1st century AD), a portrait of the owner, probably painted in his lifetime and then hung in his house, was eventually cut to shape and placed over the face of the mummy.

Other traditional tomb-goods introduced in the Middle Kingdom included models (brewers, bakers, farm workers, ships and boats) which could be made full-size and brought to life by means of magical spells, so that they could be used by the owner in the afterlife. One special group of models were

Tomb model of girl grinding corn to provide the owner with eternal food in the afterlife (c.2300 BC, Manchester Museum).

Model boat from tomb, with mummy, mourners and sailors to enable the owner to sail to Abydos (c.1900 BC, Manchester Museum).

the 'ushabtis', figurines of agricultural workers who would undertake duties for the owner in the land of Osiris, where the dead were expected to cultivate the crops. There were 365 ushabtis in each tomb group (one for each day of the year), plus twenty overseer figurines, to keep them in order.

As well as human mummies, the Egyptians also mummified many species of animals. They believed that a spark of the spirit of each of the many animal

gods they worshipped was present in each animal. Some (cult-animals) were kept at the temples, to represent the presence of those gods on earth, and these were given elaborate burials when they died. Pilgrims to the various temples and sacred sites could also purchase specially bred and reared animals and birds kept in captivity; these would be put to death, mummified and buried in mass cemeteries, as the pilgrims' offerings to the god. If they could afford to, people also undoubtedly mummified some of their pets when they died, and encased them in wooden coffins. Cats were particularly honoured in this way, as the Egyptians regarded them as protectors of their homes.

Wooden coffin for a mummified kitten, containing a carefully bandaged cat mummy (c.900 BC, Manchester Museum).

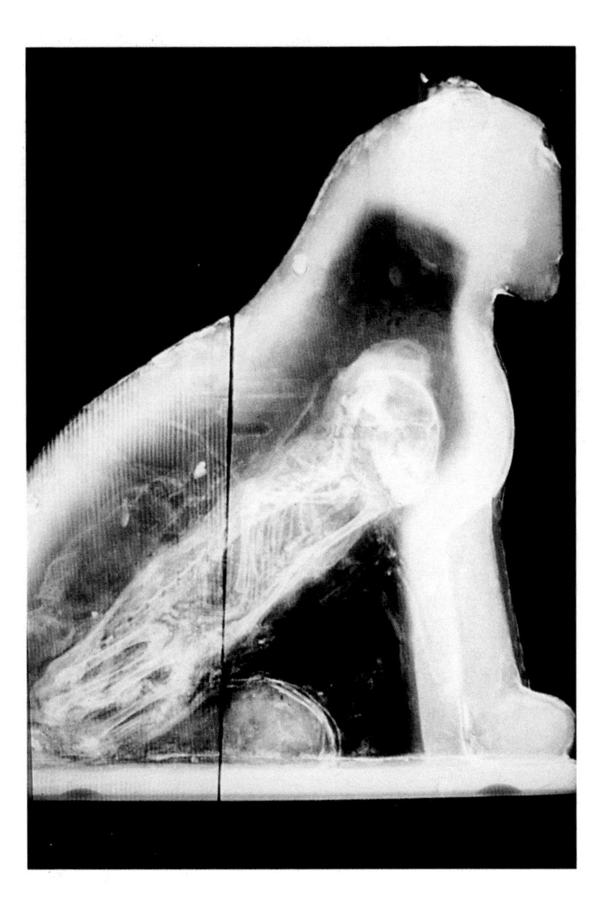

Radiograph of a mummified kitten enclosed in a wooden coffin (c.900 BC, Manchester Museum).

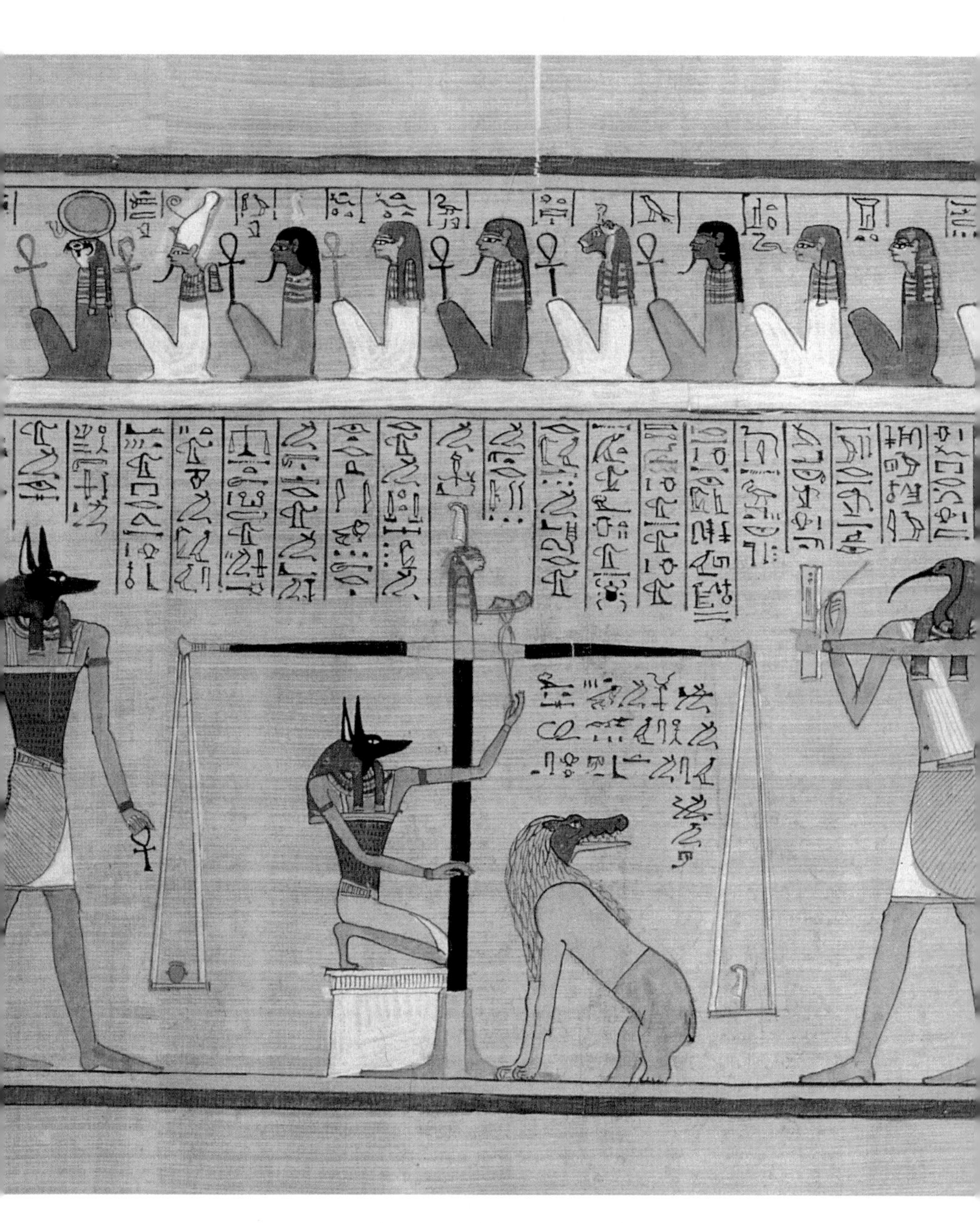

Papyrus showing weighing of the heart, when the deceased faces the god Osiris on the Day of Judgement (British Museum).

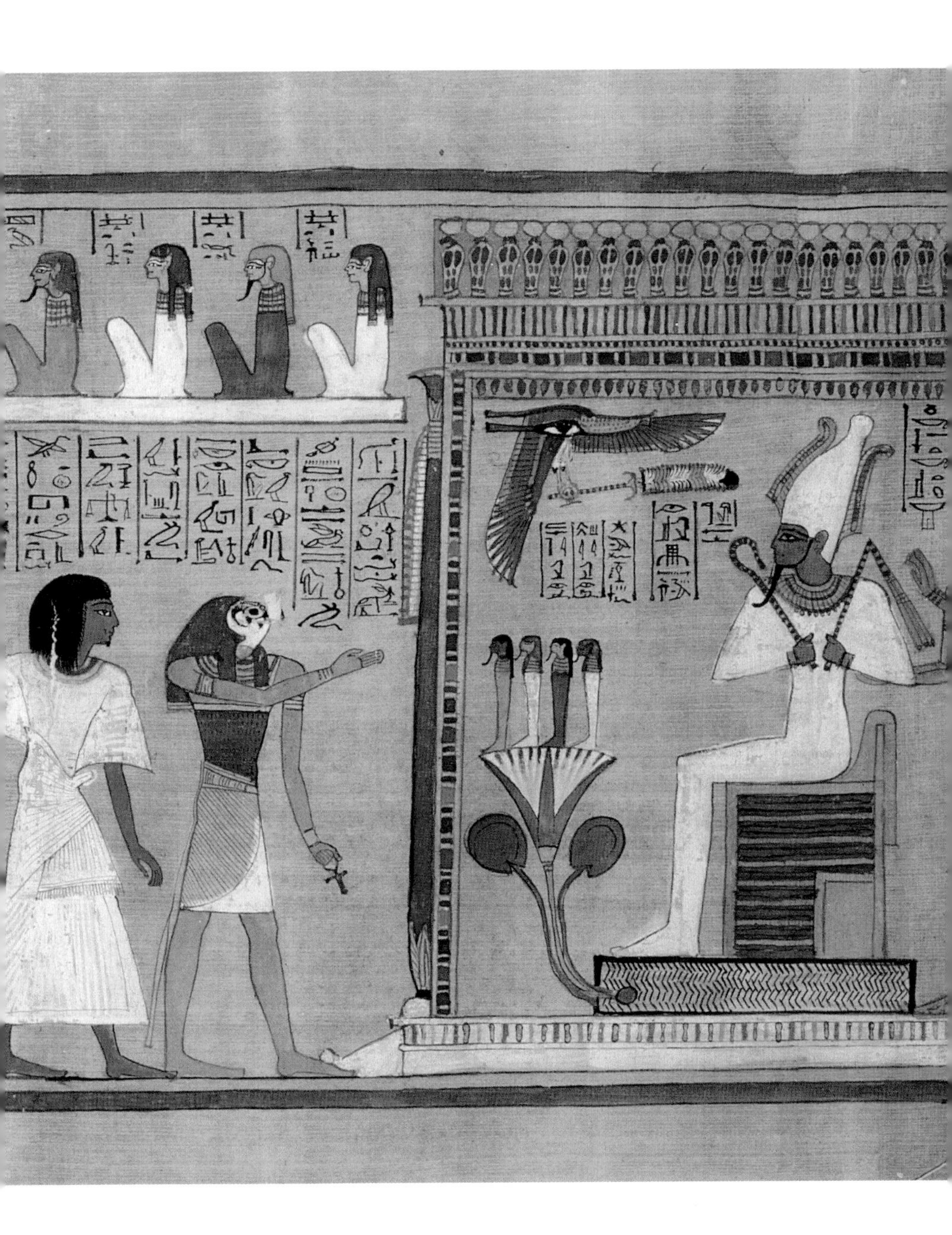

How was a mummy made?

There are no existing Egyptian texts which tell us how mummification was carried out, and there are wall scenes in only two tombs which show some of the stages in preparing and decorating the mummy. However, two Greek writers, Herodotus (5th century BC) and Diodorus Siculus (1st century BC), have left written accounts describing the main stages of the procedure, and the mummies themselves also provide us with information about the various techniques.

According to Herodotus, three main methods were available, depending on the client's ability to pay. The most expensive was the most successful in preserving the body, and involved several stages. At death, the corpse was taken by the family to the embalmer's workshop which was situated in the cemetery area. The process apparently took 70 days to complete, although perhaps only forty days were needed for the actual mummification, and religious rituals would have occupied the remaining time.

The embalmers and their assistants probably wore masks to impersonate the gods who had attended the mummification of Osiris. A special funerary priest would have presided over the various stages, and recited the relevant religious texts. First, the body was stripped and placed on a board or platform. From at least the time of the Middle Kingdom (*c.*1900 BC), the brain was removed through a passage chiselled through (usually) the left nostril and the ethmoid bone into the skull cavity. The brain tissue was then reduced to fragments by means of a metal hook which was introduced through this cavity. The embalmer used a kind of spatula to extract the fragments, but brain removal was usually incomplete and some tissue was left behind. Brain tissue, regarded as unimportant, was discarded, and the skull cavity was either left empty or later filled with resin or resin-soaked linen. Alternative measures were used in some mummies, where the brain fragments were either removed through the base of the skull or through a hole made in the eye socket. The eyes themselves were not removed; linen pads or artificial eyes made of obsidian or glass were inserted over the eyeballs, to make the mummy appear more realistic.

True mummification involved two basic processes – evisceration of the body and treatment of the tissues with natron, a substance which removed the bodily fluids. The body was eviscerated through an incision in the abdomen (usually placed on the left side). The viscera (internal organs) were reached through this incision, when the embalmer put his hand inside the abdomen to cut the organs free with a special knife. He removed them and then made a further cut in the diaphragm, so that he could pass his arm into the chest cavity. Here, he removed all the organs except the heart, which was left in place because the Egyptians believed that it was the thinking and feeling part of the person. Neither did the embalmer remove the kidneys, perhaps because they were difficult to reach. However, evisceration was rarely perfect or complete, and parts of the organs were frequently left behind. In some mummies there was no attempt at all at evisceration.

The extracted viscera were then dehydrated using natron. This substance, a mixture of sodium carbonate (washing soda) and bicarbonate (baking powder), combined with impurities, including salt, occurs in natural deposits in the Wadi en-Natrun, a dry valley in Egypt. The ancient Egyptians used natron for washing clothes and cleaning their teeth as well as for mummification.

Once treated and dried, the organs were wrapped in four parcels and placed under the protection of gods known as the Four Sons of Horus. The parcels were usually placed in four containers (Canopic jars) and kept in the tomb; some sets of jars have stoppers that represent the human, baboon, jackal and falcon heads of the Four Sons of Horus. In *c.*1000 BC a new custom was introduced, and the viscera parcels, each decorated with a wax image of the appropriate deity, were replaced in the chest and abdomen cavities of the mummy.

The next stage was to dry the body. This procedure was the equivalent of

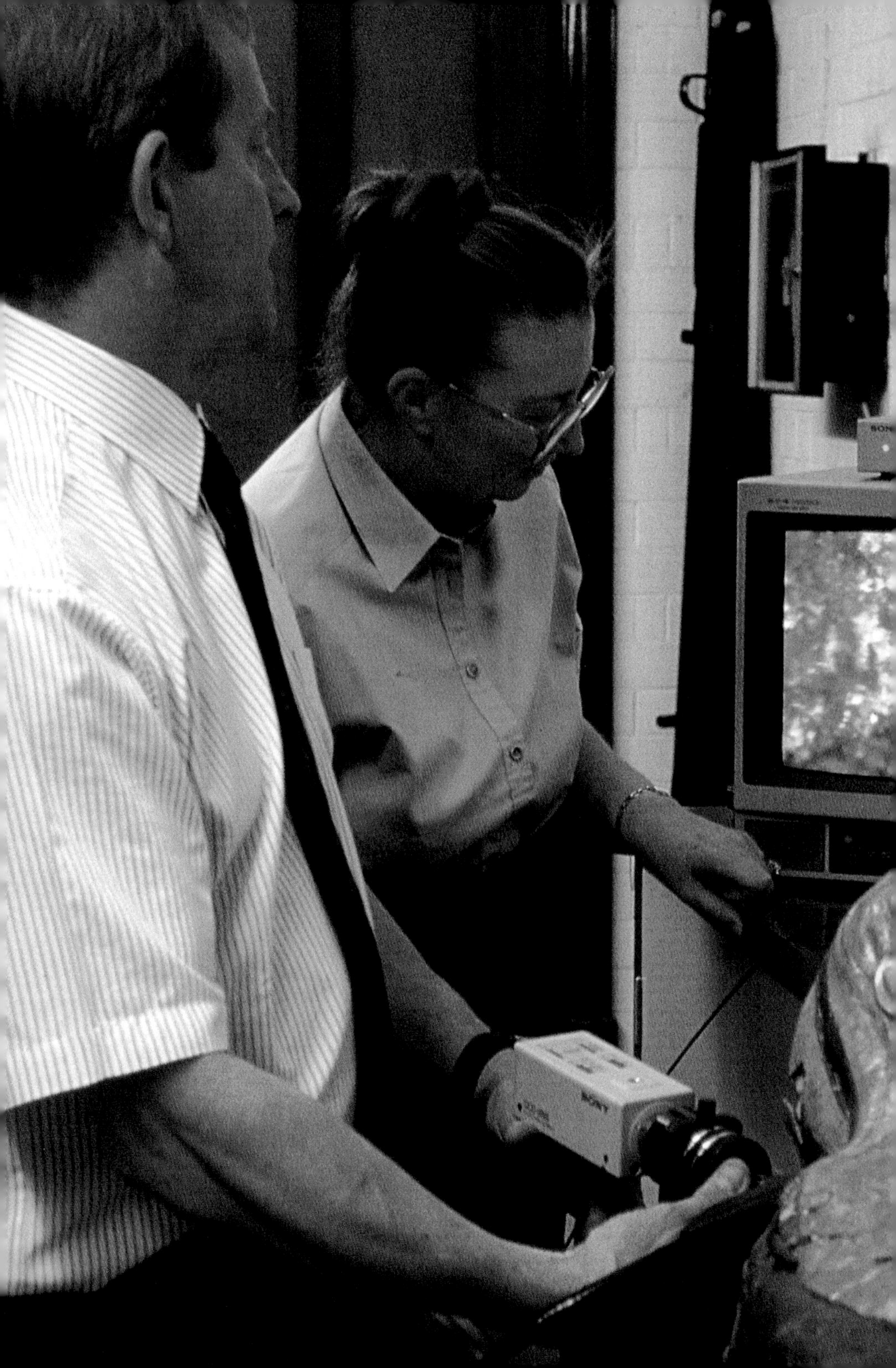

***A** view inside the mummy (shown on monitor), seen through an endoscope, a virtually non-destructive method of examination.*

modern preservative methods of embalming, involving either the injection of preserving fluids into the blood vessels, or deep freezing, or freeze-drying. Ancient techniques used either heat (sun or fire) or a dehydrating agent (natron) to remove the water content from the bodily tissues, and so prevent the growth of bacteria and the resultant decomposition of the body. In Egypt, the body was packed and covered with dry natron. This procedure, which preserved the tissues but destroyed the grease and fat, probably lasted for 40 days.

The body was then removed from the natron, and washed to remove all traces of natron and other debris. Still pliable, it was straightened out into a horizontal position so that it would fit into the coffin. During the 21st Dynasty (*c.*1000 BC), the embalmers experimented with certain refinements to

Canopic jars from the Tomb of the Two Brothers, containing mummified viscera. Rifeh, Egypt (c.1900 BC, Manchester Museum).

130
128

Wooden figurines of the four sons of Horus, gods who protected the viscera removed from the mummy (British Museum).

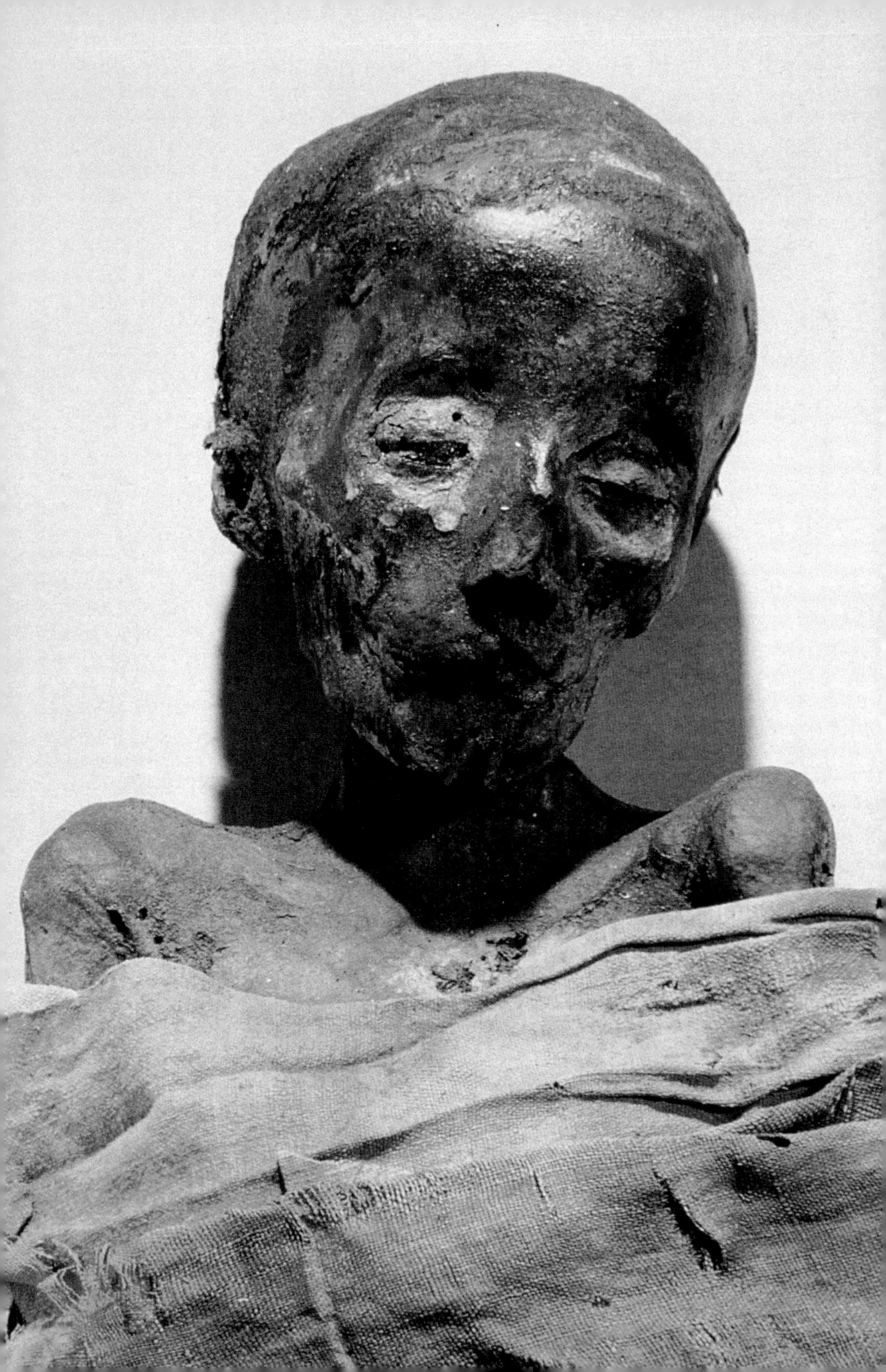

Mummy of six-year-old boy with gilded face, brought back as a souvenir from Egypt (c.1st century BC, Manchester Museum).

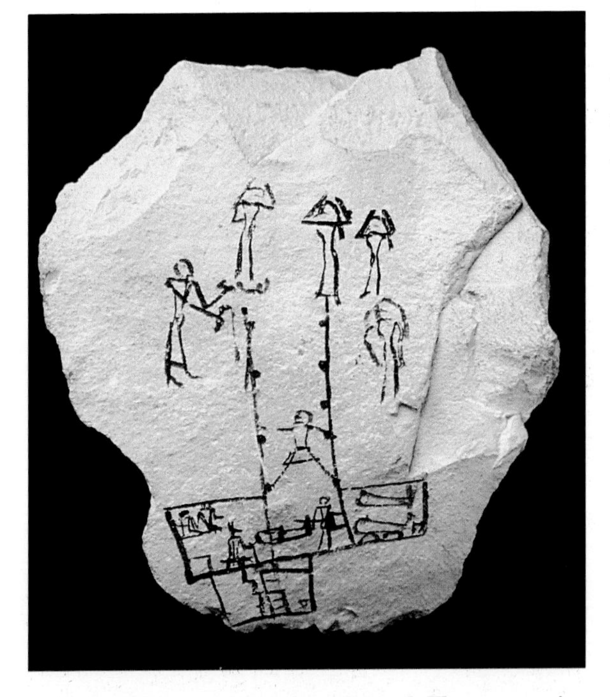

Limestone sherd showing a funeral. The mummy is lowered down the tomb-shaft into the burial chamber. Thebes (c.1400 BC, Manchester Museum).

improve the appearance of the body. To make the shrunken body appear plumper and more lifelike, the face, neck and other areas were packed with linen, sawdust, earth, sand or butter, inserted through incisions made in the skin. False eyes were added, the body surface was painted with ochre (red for men and yellow for women), and false plaits were added to the remaining natural hair.

After the body had been dehydrated and washed, it was rubbed with oils and perfumed and coated with resin, but these were only cosmetic treatments – the essential processes which preserved the body were evisceration and dehydration. Finally, the individual limbs and the body were carefully wrapped in linen bandages and cloths, and the arms were arranged either across the chest

or alongside the body. Then, in a special ceremony, a liquid or semi-liquid resin was poured over the mummy, the coffin, and the viscera in their own containers. The mummy was returned to the family, who took it, together with the dead person's funerary goods, to be placed in the tomb.

Dr Margaret Murray and her team unwrap a mummy at Manchester University in 1908, pioneering research in this field.

What can we learn from mummies today?

Because large quantities of human remains (skeletons and mummies) have survived, and since many people in Egypt today are the descendants of the ancient population (because there have been no major invasions by other races), it is now possible to study the pattern of some diseases which existed in antiquity and to see how they have developed over the centuries.

Various techniques are used by scientists to obtain evidence of disease in mummies. Radiology provides a totally non-destructive method: X-rays have

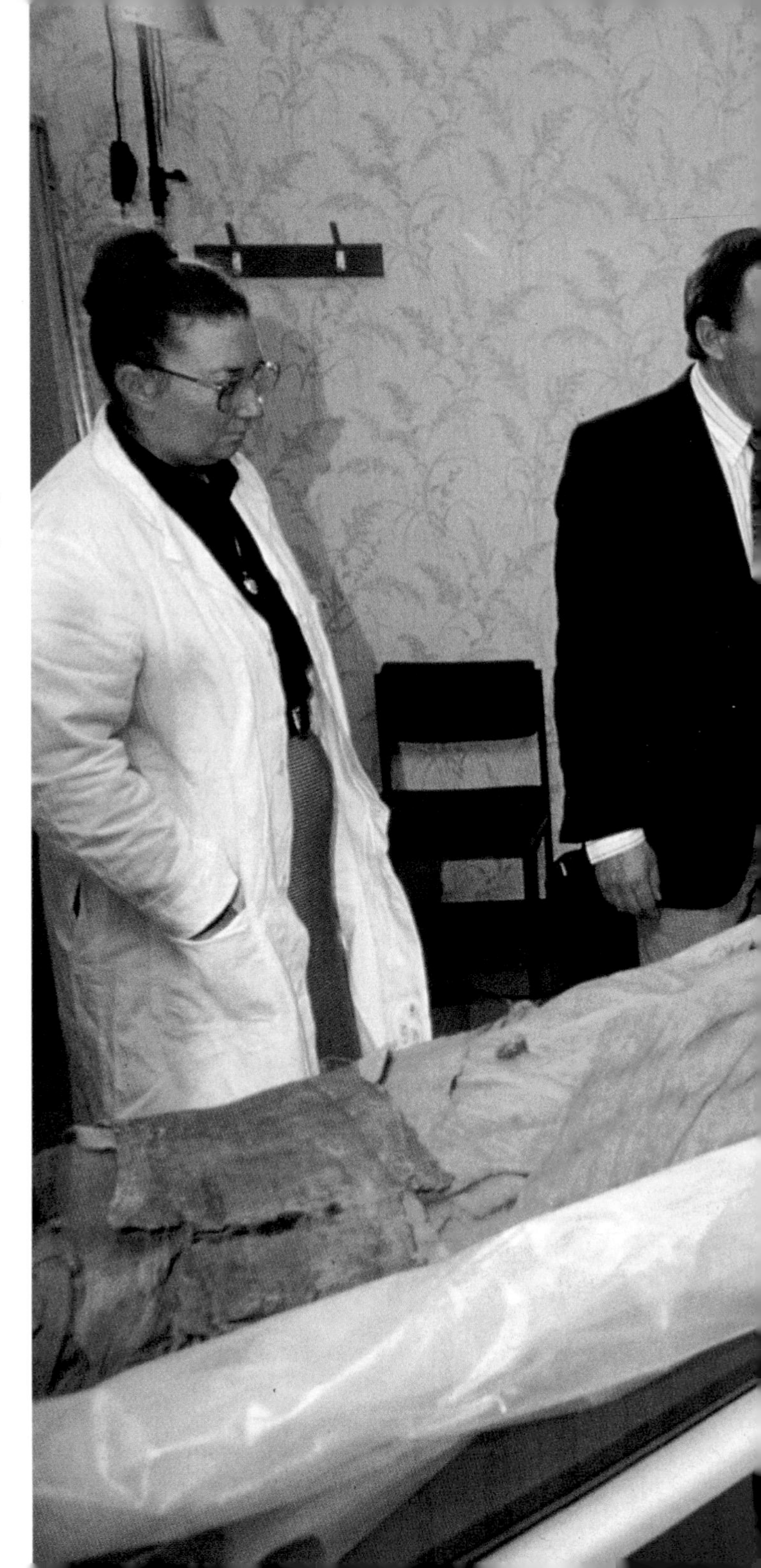

The mummy of Natsef-Amun (the Leeds Mummy) enters the CT scanner in the Medical School, University of Manchester.

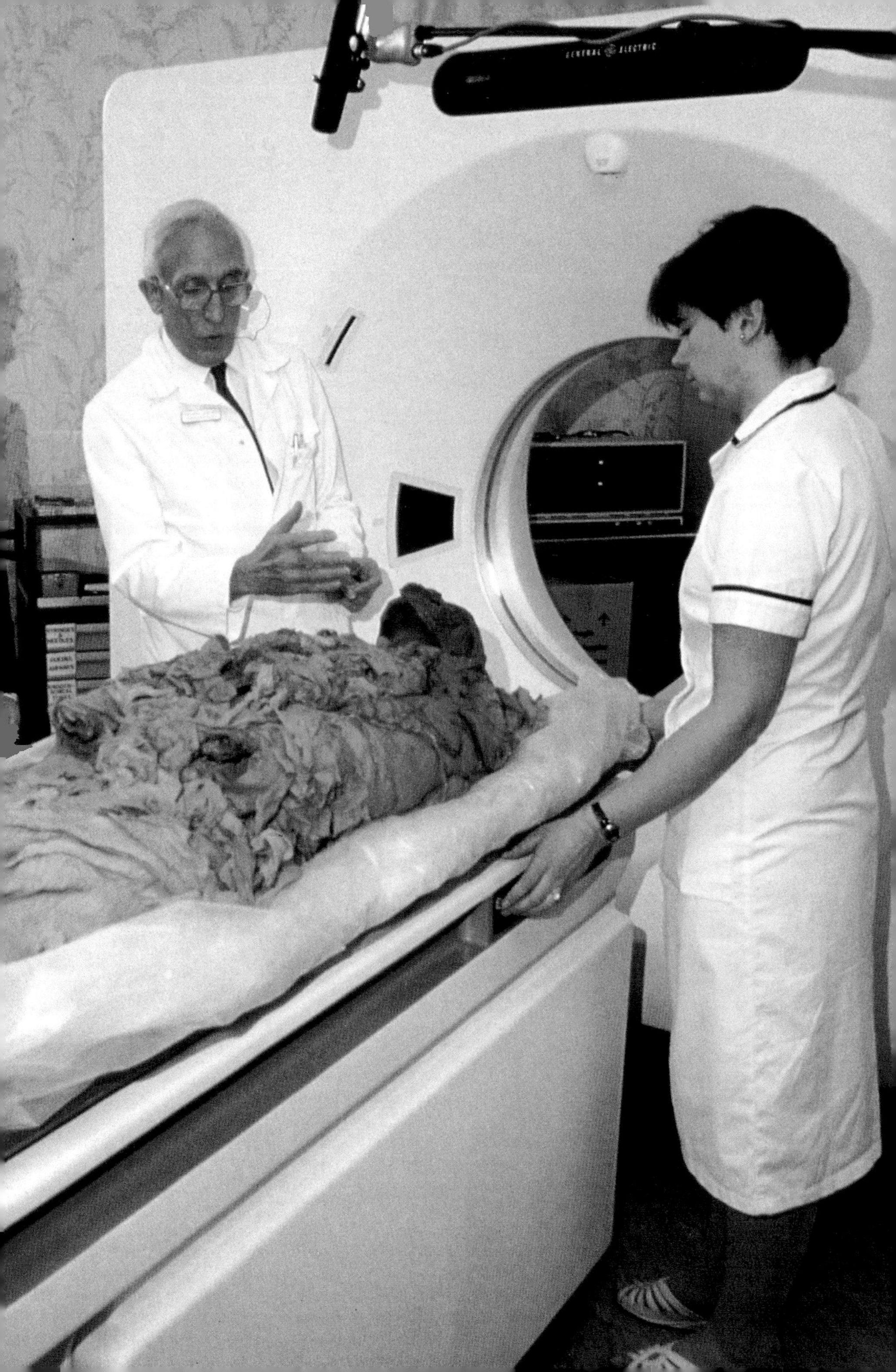
GENERAL ELECTRIC

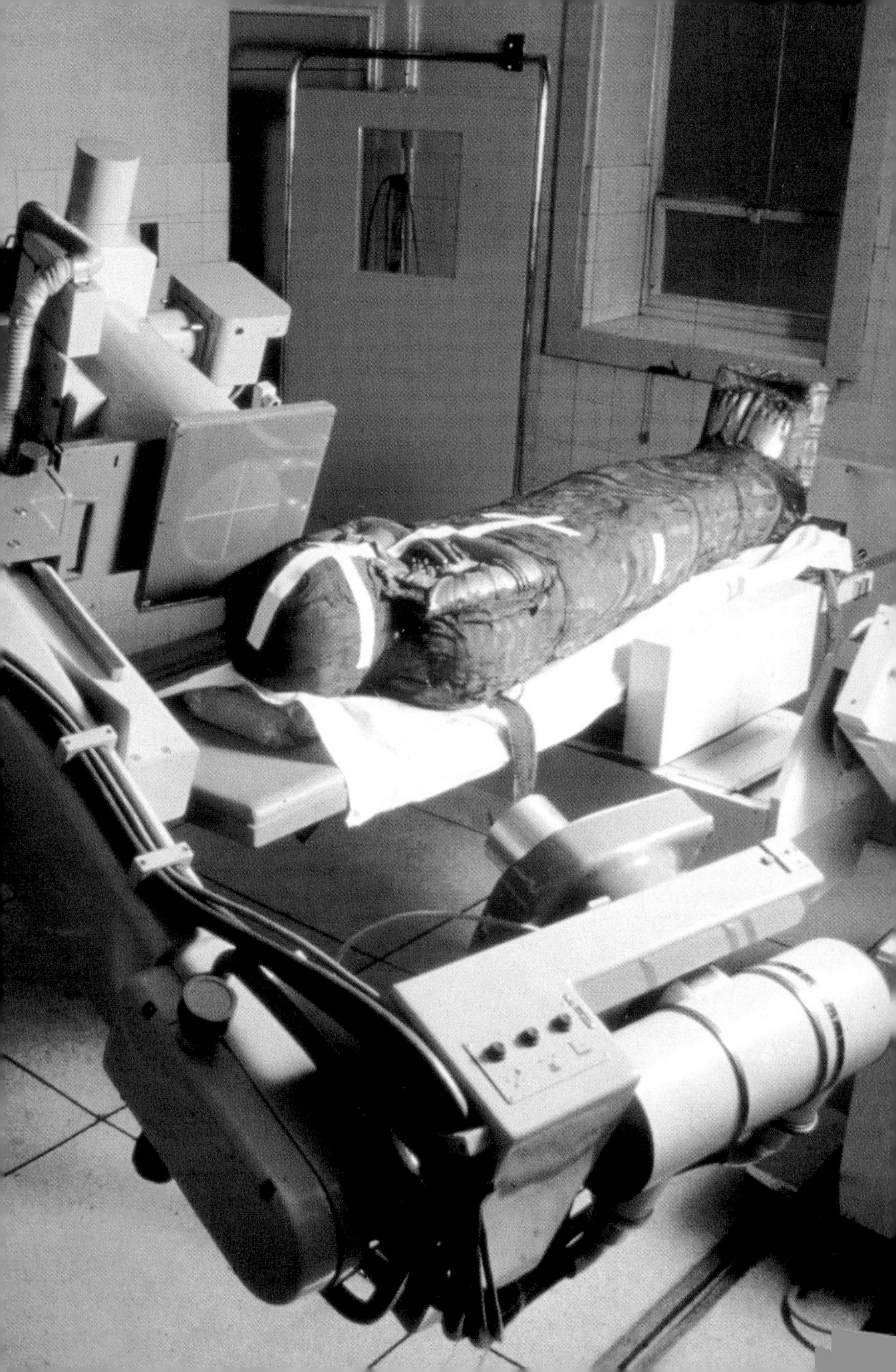

shown the presence of disease and 'wear-and-tear' injuries in the skeleton and the remaining soft tissue. Parasitic disease caused by different types of worms is common, but cancer, syphilis, tuberculosis and rickets are rare or absent.

Using an industrial endoscope, inserted through an existing hole in the mummy, samples of tissue can be removed from deep

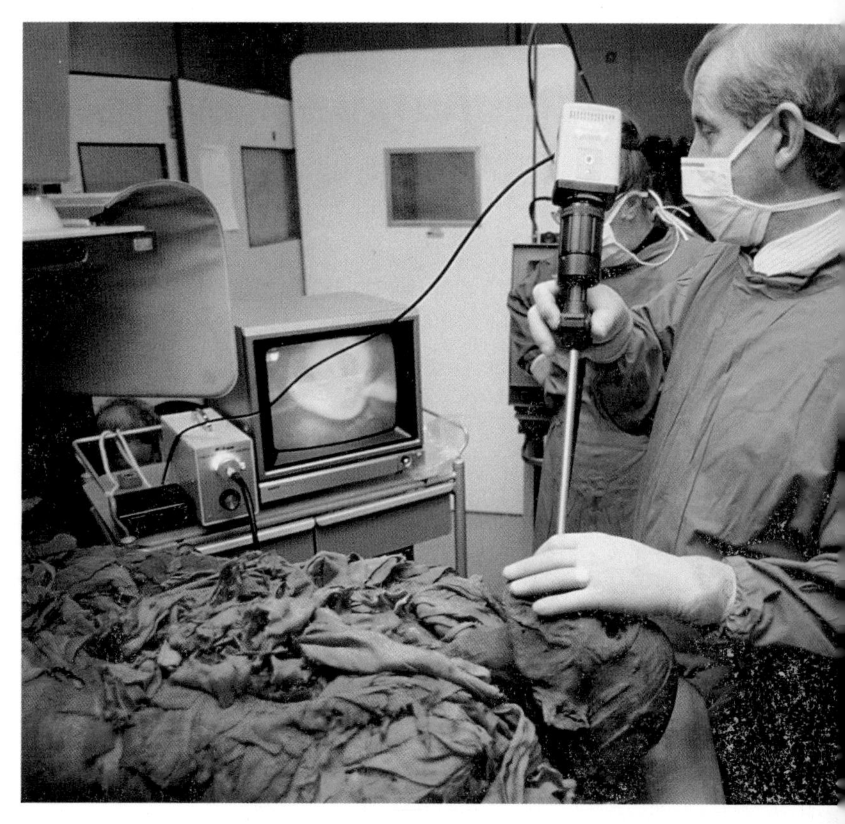

Investigation of a mummy using specialized X-ray equipment in Department of Neuro-radiology, Manchester Royal Infirmary.

Endoscopes can be used to remove tissue samples from inside mummies, for histological, immunological and genetic studies.

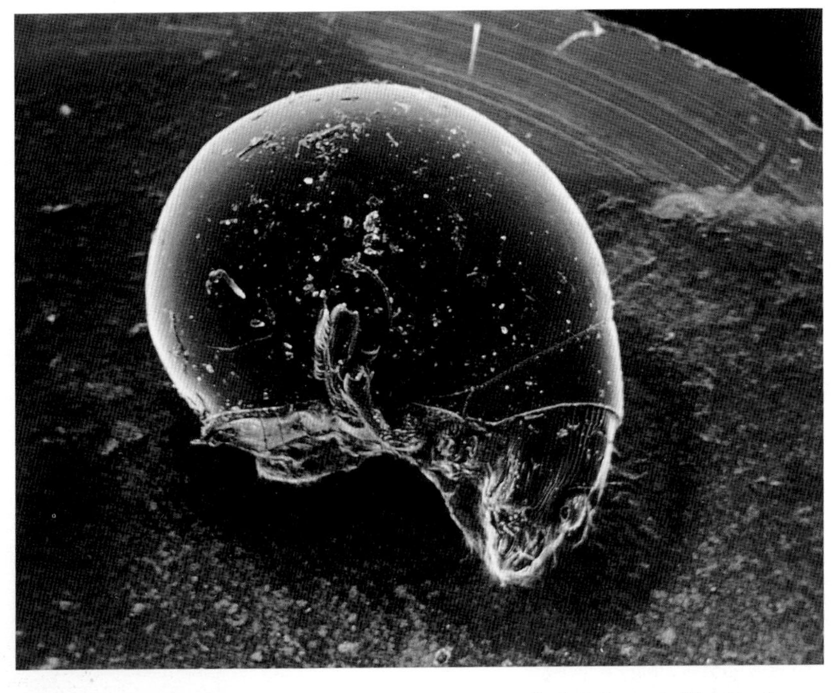

Wooden face from a coffin, with stylized features and lotus flower on head-band (c. 900 BC, Manchester Museum).

Adult hump spider beetle,* **Gibbium psylloides** *(X 36), found in mummy of Nekht-Ankh. Rifeh, Egypt (c.1900 BC).

inside the body, and sent to the laboratory where the tissue is rehydrated and then frozen, sectioned and examined under a microscope to look for evidence of disease. An endoscope (a narrow metal tube with a light source) allows the user to look down one end and view the contents of the mummy; it also permits the researcher to gain almost non-destructive access to the mummy. This method has replaced the destructive autopsies of mummies which took place in earlier years.

Tissue obtained in this way can also be used for genetic studies. Techniques developed to identify DNA in mummified tissue now enable studies of family

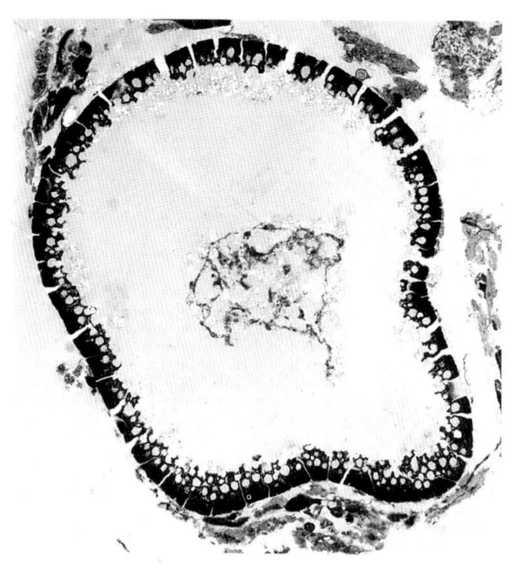

Section through intestinal wall showing remains of a parasitic worm (X 3000). From mummy of Asru, a temple singer (c.900 BC).

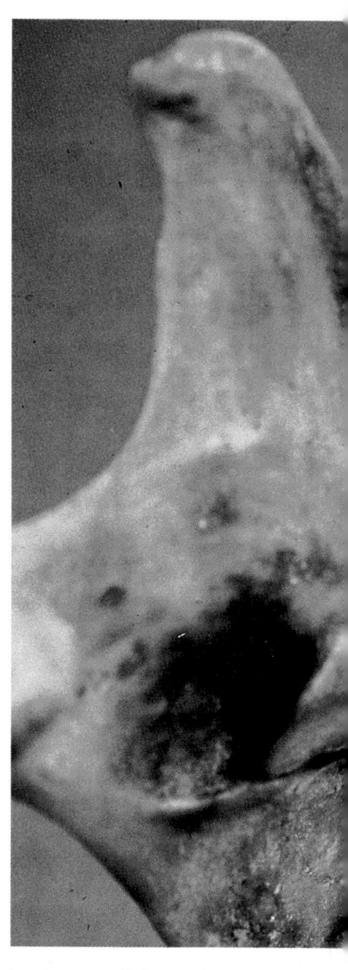

Lower jaw of Khnum-Nakht, showing severe dental attrition caused by grit and sand in the bread (c.1900 BC).

relationships to be undertaken. In future, it may also be possible to find evidence of bacterial, fungal and viral DNA in mummies, indicating that an individual had suffered from a particular infectious disease.

There have also been several important studies on the dental health and diet of the ancient Egyptians, and we now know that, although caries (tooth decay) was quite rare, they did suffer from severe wear of the biting surfaces of the teeth. This was the result of their diet: bread was the most popular food, and samples of bread found in tombs which have been examined show that it was

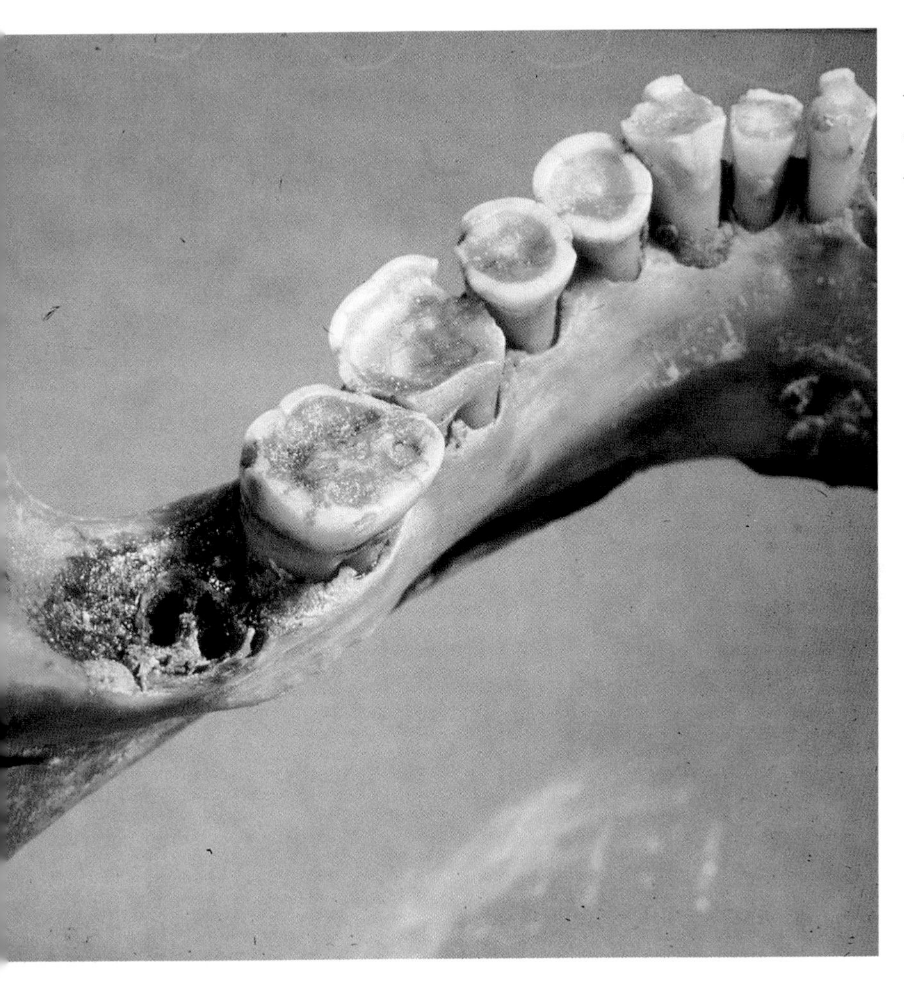

heavily contaminated by windblown sand and grit from grinding the corn. By the time they reached adolescence, most people had suffered some degree of dental wear, and the problem progressed as they became older.

By studying the mummies using these scientific techniques, we can gain a more accurate picture of their lifestyle. It is clear that they suffered from a wide range of diseases and health problems which must have affected their enjoyment of life, and this evidence must be set against the 'glamorous' image of ancient Egypt depicted in their paintings, sculpture, and literature.

PHOTOGRAPHIC ACKNOWLEDGEMENTS
All pictures from The Manchester Museum with the exception of cover Archiv für Kunst und Geschichte London [AKG]; pages 2, 5 E.T. Archive; pp. 6–7 AKG; pp. 8–9c The British Museum; pp. 18–19.

First published in Great Britain 1997
by George Weidenfeld and Nicolson Ltd
The Orion Publishing Group
5 Upper St Martin's Lane
London WC2H 9EA

A CIP catalogue record for this book is available from the British Library
ISBN 0297 823159

Picture Research: Joanne King

Designed by Harry Green

Typeset in Baskerville